FUN WITH SCIENCE

CYCLES AND SEASONS

ROSIE HARLOW & GARETH MORGAN

Contents

Use the symbols below to help you
identify the three kinds of practical
activities in this book.

EXPERIMENTS   GAMES   THINGS TO MAKE

Illustrated by Kuo Kang Chen · Liz Peperell and Oxford Illustrators

WARWICK PRESS

Introduction

As our planet earth circles around the Sun each year, the weather changes in a seasonal pattern. During the warm months of Summer, more sunlight energy reaches the surface of the earth than in the cold Winter months. The closer you live to the North (or South) Pole the more pronounced this change is. Many plants and animals have a way of life that follows this yearly pattern of the seasons.

In this book you will find experiments to help you discover for yourself how living things adapt to the changing seasons. The first two pages in each section look at the weather typical of the season. Following that, you will find experiments exploring the way in which animals and plants respond to the season. Concluding each section you will find activities that use natural materials of the season.

The seasons are not clear cut like days or months. For example, there are often warm weeks in the middle of Winter. In some years, Summer takes a long time to arrive. Because of this you will find that many of the experiments from one season may be done at other times of the year.

WARNING!

Many plants are extremely poisonous and should not be eaten. Always check with an adult before you try any experiments which involve cooking or eating flowers, leaves, berries or fungi.

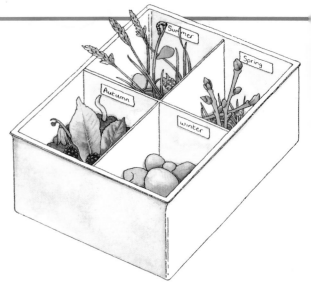

▲ What is weather and what are the seasons? (pages 4 and 5)

▲ What happens to trees through the year? (pages 9, 17, 25, and 33)

▼ How can you record and forecast the weather? (pages 4, 5, 15, and 23)

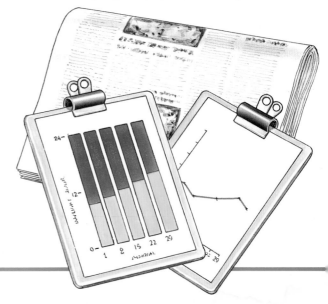

▼ How do plants survive the seasons? (pages 8, 16, 17, 24, and 25)

▲ What happens to plants in extreme conditions? (pages 8 and 24)

▲ How can you make tasty seasonal snacks from wild plants? (pages 20, 21, and 35)

▲ How can you capture the colors of the seasons? (pages 12, 15, 20, 21, and 29)

▼ Taking a lesson from Nature, how can you recycle your garbage? (pages 32 and 36)

▲ Animals survive the seasons: how do animals find food and stay warm? (pages 6, 7, 10 and 11)

What Season is it?

Look around outside. What season is it? Sometimes it is easy to decide. You will be able to make up your mind by looking at the weather and what is happening in the natural world. However, you may have a problem deciding which season it is. To help you, these two pages contain information about the weather and the seasons.

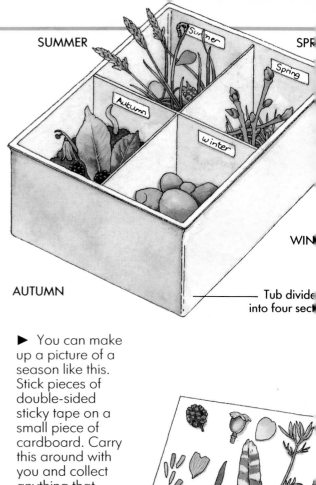

SUMMER
SPR
AUTUMN
WIN

Tub divide
into four sec

The Four Season Box

To help you decide which season it is, make a four season box. Divide a plastic box into four sections as shown, using cardboard and sticky tape. Label the sections Spring, Summer, Autumn, and Winter. Now look around outside for things that make you think of any one of the seasons, and put them in that section of the box. For example, a fallen leaf might remind you of Autumn, or a flower petal of Spring. If you see something that is too big to go in the box (perhaps somebody in a woolly hat makes you think of Winter), write it down on a piece of paper to put in the box. The section that fills up fastest will probably be the season that you are in at the moment.

▶ You can make up a picture of a season like this. Stick pieces of double-sided sticky tape on a small piece of cardboard. Carry this around with you and collect anything that indicates to you the season that you are in.

Double-sided sticky tape

The Spirit of the Season

Each season has a different "feel." To capture the spirit of the season go to your favorite outdoors place, or sit by an open window with a sheet of paper and a pencil. Make yourself comfortable then close your eyes and listen. Now look around. How do your surroundings feel and smell? Write down words as they come to mind. Now cut the words up and arrange them to make sense, adding joining words. Your "poem" will capture the spirit of the season.

FRESH   FROST   SPARKLE
BLACK   SKELETONS CRISP
SHARP   COLD   HARD
CLOUDS   WHITE   WIND

CLOUDS LIKE WHITE SKELE
SHADE THE SHARP BLACK EA

Windy Weather

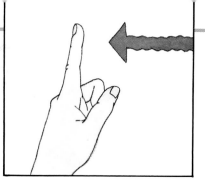

The strength of the wind, and where it blows from, will affect the weather. Wind blowing in from the sea may bring rain. Wind from the south might bring hot weather. Here is an easy way to find out which way the wind is blowing from. Lick the pad of one finger and hold it above your head. When the finger is facing the wind it will feel cool. Use a compass, or ask someone, to find out which direction this is. Use these pictures showing the Beaufort Scale of wind speeds to work out how strong the wind is.

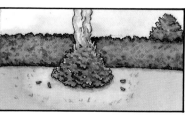

Force 0 Calm: leaves don't even stir.

Force 1–3 Light breeze: leaves and twigs start to move.

Force 4–5 Moderate wind: small trees start to sway.

Force 6–7 Strong wind: big trees sway.

Force 8–9 Gale: branches blown off.

Force 10–12 Storm and hurricane: trees are blown over.

Nature's Forecasters

The seasons and the weather affect plants and animals. For centuries people have used these reactions to forecast the weather. For example, the mistle thrush is known as the "storm cock" because it often sings from a treetop in windy weather. The arrival of the swallows means that summer is on the way—but one swallow does not make a summer! Here are some other sayings that have developed from observing plants and animals:

"When the swallows fly high, it will be dry."
"If the cows are lying down it will rain."
"A good Autumn for fruit means a hard Winter to come."

See if you can find some more weather sayings, and test them to see if they are true.

Swallow

Thrush

Winter

In the north, Winter is a cold time of short days and long nights. For many animals and plants life is hard. They must survive until the warmer weather arrives. Their survival will depend on how well prepared they are, and how severe the Winter is. Find out in this section what weather is in store for them, and how they will survive it.

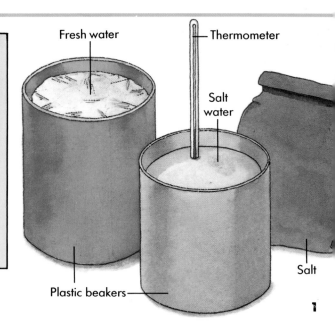

Fresh water
Thermometer
Salt water
Salt
Plastic beakers
1

Freezing Water

1. When the temperature falls below 32°F water freezes from a liquid into a solid. Put a plastic cup of water into the freezer. Check the temperature of the water at intervals to see at what temperature the ice starts to form. Repeat the experiment, but add salt to the water first. Salty water, such as the sea, stays liquid even below 32°F.

2. Fill a container with fresh snow. Level off the snow, but don't press it down. Leave the snow to melt, then look to see how much water is left. Snow takes up more space than water, chiefly because it contains a lot of air. The space between the top of the melted water and the top of the container shows you roughly how much air there was in the snow.

Snow
Melted snow
Plastic beakers
2

Life under the Snow

Because snow contains so much air, it is a good insulator. This means that it acts like a blanket and helps warm things to stay warm! The snow also helps to protect plants from damage by the cold winds and frosts. For animals that cannot bury themselves under the snow life is more difficult. Deer cannot find plants to eat; owls and stoats must search for the small mammals they need to eat for energy. To stop using up valuable energy, some animals hibernate in the Winter.

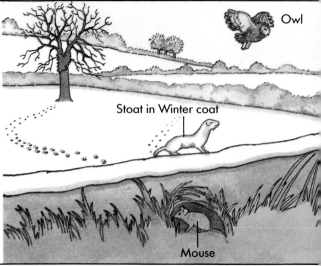

Owl
Stoat in Winter coat
Mouse

Life under the Ice

In the experiment opposite you will observe that as ice starts to form it floats on top of the water. A layer of ice on a pond has the same effect as a layer of snow on the ground; it helps to insulate the water underneath, so that it takes longer for the rest of the water to freeze. Plants under the ice layer are not damaged, and fish can also survive. However, this is no help to ducks. They cannot reach the water and have to migrate elsewhere.

▲ Water in the air condenses as the temperature falls. In cold weather the water forms crystals of ice and often appears as white "hoar frost." Each crystal has perfect six-sided symmetry like a snowflake.

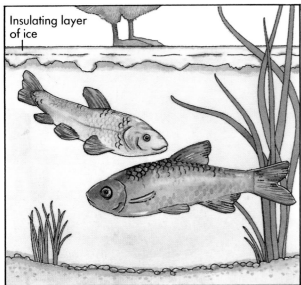

Insulating layer of ice

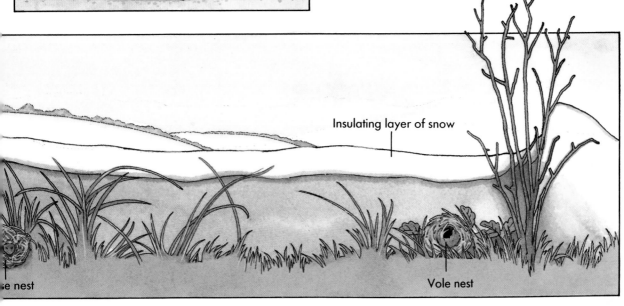

Insulating layer of snow

e nest

Vole nest

A Winter Wander

Many plants die back in the Winter because they are too delicate to survive the frost. However, some are well suited to the harsh conditions, and will even flower. Take a walk on a warm Winter's day and see if any flowers are out. Look to see if they are in the sun or in the shade. Plants that flower in cold temperatures often have tough and waxy leaves to stop them drying out.

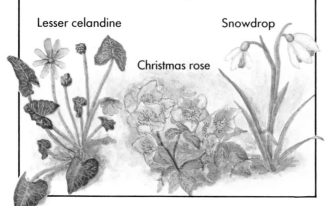

Lesser celandine

Snowdrop

Christmas rose

Trees in Winter

A tree needs to make food to stay alive. The food is made in the leaves, using sunlight energy to make sugars by a process called **photosynthesis** . At the same time water is lost from the leaves, and the tree must replace this water by absorbing fresh water from the soil into its roots. During Winter, less sunlight is available to make food. At the same time the water in the soil becomes frozen, so it cannot

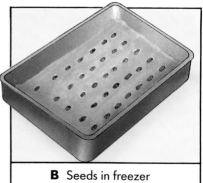

Evergreen twig

Deciduous twig

Plants in the Cold

Do this experiment to find out what happens to plants when the temperature falls below freezing. Put cress seeds on damp tissue paper in two plastic trays. Place container A in a warm closet and container B in a freezer. Water the seeds when the paper feels dry and wait to see which seeds grow roots and shoots. Prepare two more trays in the same way, but put both containers in a warm closet and leave them to germinate for a few days. Then leave container C in the closet, but move D into a freezer. You will be able to watch the effect of the cold on the young seedlings.

A Seeds in warm cupboard

B Seeds in freezer

C Seedlings in warm cupboard

D Seedlings in freezer

be absorbed. If a tree kept losing water through its leaves it would dry out. Look for a **deciduous** twig like the one shown. Deciduous trees lose their leaves in the Winter. The leaves for next year are safe inside the bud. Compare this with a twig from an **evergreen** tree which keeps its leaves in the Winter. The leaves are tough and waxy. They lose only a small amount of water, so the tree can keep them without drying out.

Compare these pictures of a silver birch in Summer and in Winter. Then look at the Wintertime trees shown below. Which of these are deciduous and which are evergreen?

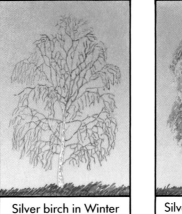
Silver birch in Winter

Silver birch in Summer

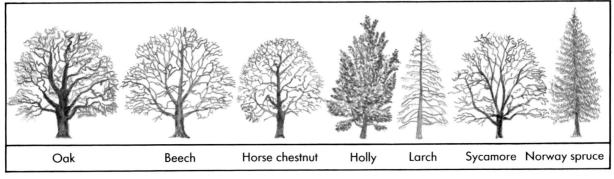

| Oak | Beech | Horse chestnut | Holly | Larch | Sycamore | Norway spruce |

This is an oak tree in Winter. The oak is a deciduous tree: it sheds its leaves for the Winter months. A bare tree like this is sometimes called a tree skeleton. Water is lost through the leaves of a tree by transpiration, so by losing its leaves, the tree saves water. However, without leaves the tree cannot make the food it needs to grow. The tree is dormant in Winter—it stops growing and it needs very little energy to stay alive. To find out what happens to the fallen leaves, see page 33. To find out more about what leaves do, look at page 25.

Keeping Warm

Animals face some of the same problems in Winter as plants do. Water may be difficult to find. Food for energy is in short supply. In addition, warm-blooded creatures must conserve heat. Air is a good insulator and reduces the loss of heat. Humans wear layers of clothing (*see the picture to the right*). Many mammals increase the thickness of their fur, and birds fluff out their feathers to create an insulating layer of air around their bodies. People can turn up the heating in their homes — but animals have to generate their own heat by eating enough of the right foods.

The Survival Game

Mammals require certain things to survive the Winter. For example, they need food, shelter, water, and bedding. Write down these, and any others you can think of on a sheet of paper and cut each word out. Poke a toothpick through each one to make a flag. Choose a small area outside and see if you can find all the requirements for survival for one particular animal, for example, a mouse. If you find suitable food (perhaps seeds) mark it with the food flag, and so on. Repeat the game for different animals, and set a time limit. Sometimes you will not be able to find all the requirements. Imagine what would happen to the animal if this happened in real life.

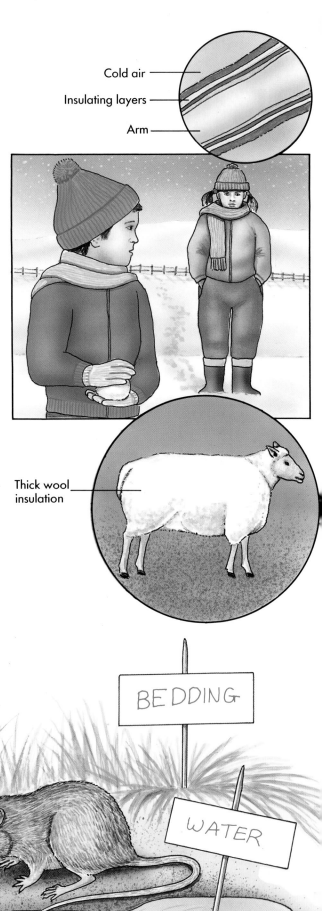

Cold air

Insulating layers

Arm

Thick wool insulation

SHELTER

FOOD

BEDDING

WATER

It's a Bird's Life

Like mammals, birds find it hard to find enough food to stay alive in the Winter. You can demonstrate this by collecting natural bird foods outside. Try to fill a matchbox. Do the experiment in different areas, and repeat it in different weather conditions. You can help birds to survive by putting out food, such as seeds, crusts and nuts, and water — away from cats (*see page 13*). Birds will feed on a wide windowsill. Do not put out moldy foods, desiccated coconut or very salty foods. Dry food should be soaked first.

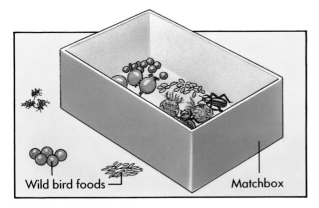

Wild bird foods ⌐   Matchbox

Dozy Minibeasts

The temperature of most mammals and birds is kept constantly high, but the temperature of many other creatures rises and falls with the temperature of their surroundings. When it is cold their temperature drops and they become slow and dozy. This state is called **hibernation**. Hibernating creatures do very little, so they need little energy to stay alive. This means they do not need to eat—they can use stored energy. Look for hibernating minibeasts, but take care not to disturb them or they will waste vital energy. Search under rotten wood and in sheds. Some types of animal change their form completely in the Winter. Adult insects often cannot survive in very cold conditions. Look instead for the egg or the pupa stages of the insect life cycle.

Hungry Owls

Try your luck as a hungry owl in this game. You will need a supply of counters to represent units of energy. At the beginning of the game the owl has a reserve of ten counters stored as fat. Each week she uses up three counters of energy to stay alive. Take these away at the beginning of each round, then throw a die to find out how many voles the owl catches during the week. For each vole caught, add one counter to the owl. The owl cannot store more than ten units of energy, so if you catch more voles than there is room for, put the extra counters back. Does your owl ever run out of energy, and die? Play the game again in "Winter conditions." Many of the voles are now hidden under the snow. Only four voles can be caught each week, so even if you throw a five or six you can add only four counters to the owl. How many weeks does the owl survive?

Make a cardboard owl

Counters represent units of energy

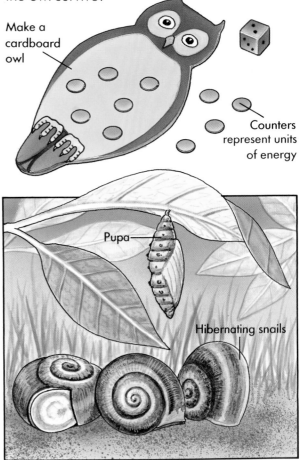

Pupa

Hibernating snails

Christmas Decorations

1. Fill a wide-necked bottle with water and rest a hyacinth bulb in the top. The base of the bulb should just touch the top of the water. Keep the bulb somewhere dark while it sprouts. Then bring the plant into the light to allow it to turn green and develop a flower.

2. Stretch two wire clothes hangers into circles. Lie one on top of the other. Weave long strands of ivy around the circles of wire so that they are bound together. Stick other evergreen branches, such as holly and any other decorations into the circle.

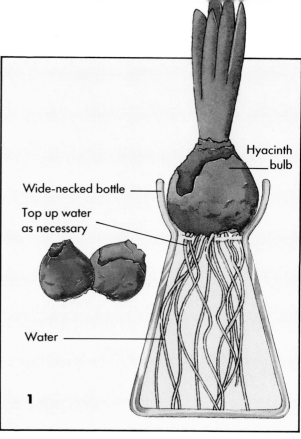

Hyacinth bulb

Wide-necked bottle

Top up water as necessary

Water

1

Wire hangers

Holly

Ivy

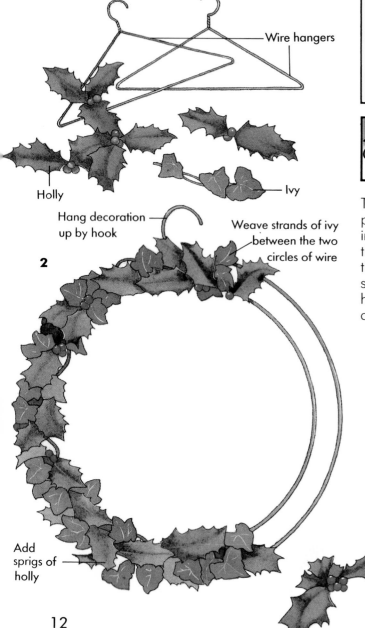

Hang decoration up by hook

Weave strands of ivy between the two circles of wire

Add sprigs of holly

2

Making Snowflakes

Trace around a plate to make a circle on a piece of paper, and cut it out. Fold the paper in half. The semicircle formed must be folded in thirds, as shown, to form a cone six layers thick. Now cut pieces out along the edges with scissors. When the paper is unfolded you will have a symmetrical snowflake. Snowflakes always have six-sided symmetry.

Fold paper here

Feed the Birds

Coconut

Peanuts

Many animals, including birds, find it difficult to find food during the Winter months. You can help by feeding them (*see page 11*). Making and hanging up a string of peanuts will provide you with entertainment, as the more acrobatic birds try to get the nuts out. Ask an adult to help you thread the nuts together with a strong needle.

▼ Even in Winter, preparations are underway for Spring. Take a Winter walk and see if you can see any early flowers, or birds pairing up.

Make a Plastercast

Plastercast

Mammal and bird footprints in snow soon disappear, but if you find prints in mud you can make a permanent record. Cut a two-inch-wide strip of thin cardboard. Make it into a circle just bigger than the print. Tape it firmly, then push it into the ground around the print. Make up some plaster of paris, stirring until it is creamy. Quickly pour it onto the print, before it becomes solid. Take the cast home when it is hard to touch and remove the cardboard when the plaster is completely hard. If you paint the plaster print you can make animal tracks on paper.

Cardboard

Plaster of Paris

Print in mud

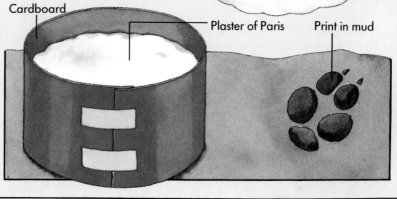

Spring

During the Spring the days quickly become longer. Many plants and animals remain dormant until the increased light and warmth trigger them into action. Often they are waiting for the days to reach a certain length before they stir into activity. Then animals prepare to breed, and plants begin to sprout. The longer days also bring a number of changes in the weather.

Spring Showers

Spring tends to be a showery time of year. Rain is part of the **water cycle**. Water on the surface of the earth (for example, in the sea or in the soil) turns into vapor, or **evaporates** into the air. To find out why evaporation is faster in the Spring, try this experiment.

Pour the same amount of water into two identical saucers. Place one saucer on a sunny, warm windowsill and the other in the refrigerator. Look each day to see which evaporates most quickly. More water evaporates in the warm Spring than in the cold Winter. To find out what happens to evaporated water, breathe onto a cold mirror

or window. The water in your warm breath condenses as it meets the cold glass.

When warm air containing evaporated water blows over cold land, clouds form and rain falls. This is why Spring tends to be showery.

In the warm

In the refrigerator

Be a Rain Forecaster

The combination of Spring rain and warm sunshine helps plants to grow. There are a number of signs in nature that are supposed to forecast the coming of rain. You can test some of these old methods to see which work:

A piece of seaweed hung outside becomes wet.
A pine cone closes up.
The scarlet pimpernel flower is known as the "poor man's weather glass" because it closes up if bad weather is on the way.

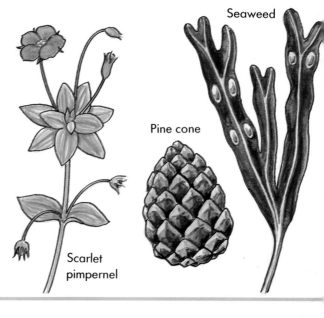

Seaweed

Pine cone

Scarlet pimpernel

The Color of the Season

Cut out different colors from an old magazine. Take the colors outside and see which of them you can match exactly with the natural things around. Keep the colors that match in a separate box. When you have matched ten colors, look in the box. These are the colors of nature in Spring. You can try this game in different seasons. Spring tends to be a time of light greens. In Autumn you are more likely to find reds and browns.

Colored squares

Warmer Days

On the same day every week, look up the maximum temperature for your area in a newspaper. Mark it onto a graph for eight weeks and you will see the overall pattern of temperature in Spring. To make your graph, draw two lines on squared paper at right angles. On the bottom line mark the dates on which you looked up the temperatures. On the line up the side mark a scale of temperatures 32–90°F.

You can also check how quickly the days lengthen during Spring by making a bar chart. Look up the sunset and sunrise hours in the paper once a week. You can then work out the number of daylight hours in each 24 hours.

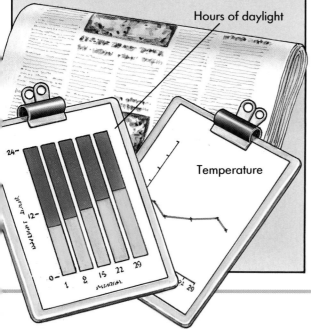

Hours of daylight

Temperature

The Last Frost

The date of the last frost is important to plants. A late Spring frost will destroy many of the new buds. Some farmers light fires near their fruit trees to stop this happening. To find the date of the last frost put a container of water outside each night. If a layer of ice has formed in the morning, note the date. Even better, leave out an upturned trash can lid as a bird bath, and check that. Remember to remove the ice to let the birds have their bath!

Ice

A Head Start

Plants must make use of the increasing sunlight energy in the Spring to make food by photosynthesis. The time at which they start to grow is critical. If they start too early they may be killed by frost. If they start too late deciduous trees may have come into leaf overhead, cutting out the vital sunlight energy. Plants growing from seeds will be slow to develop because they have to make all their own food as they grow. However, many plants store food over the Winter. This means that they have a head start in the Spring as they use the stored food to push their way up through the soil. During the rapid growth of the plant much of the stored food energy is used up. This must be replaced later. Some of the food made in the leaves by photosynthesis will be returned to the underground stems. In this way, the cycle can continue again next year.

The food is sometimes stored in bulbs, which are really swollen leaves. Bluebells and ramsons (wild garlic) store their food in this way. In other plants the food is stored in underground stems, for example celandines, violets, and primroses. Look in flowerbeds where pets or squirrels have been digging to see which plants have food stored beneath the soil.

Trees in Spring

Deciduous trees in Spring and Winter can be identified by their shape (see page 9). It is also possible to identify them by looking at the buds. To identify a twig you will need to answer these questions. What shape are the buds (for example, pointed or round)? What color are they? Are they in pairs, or do they alternate along the twig?

Mark a twig with some colored thread. Look at the buds and write down what you think the tree is. Observe your twig each week until it comes into leaf, when you can identify it by its leaves. How many trees can you identify correctly by looking at the buds?

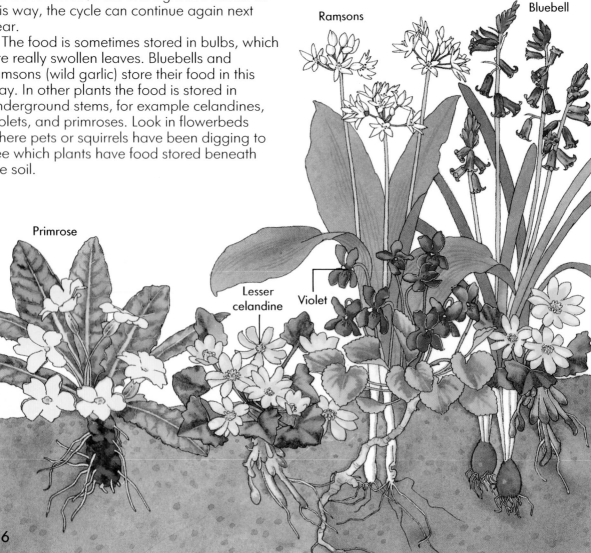

Ramsons

Bluebell

Primrose

Lesser celandine

Violet

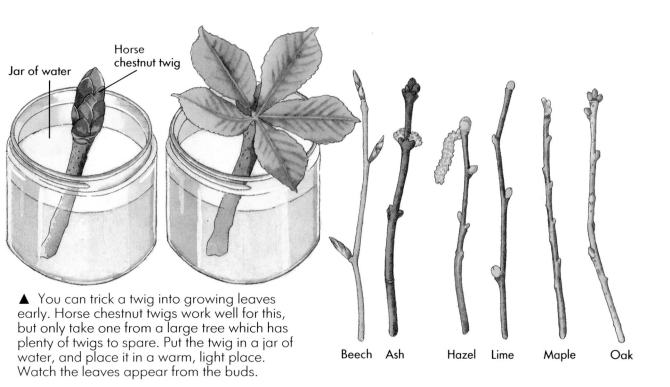

▲ You can trick a twig into growing leaves early. Horse chestnut twigs work well for this, but only take one from a large tree which has plenty of twigs to spare. Put the twig in a jar of water, and place it in a warm, light place. Watch the leaves appear from the buds.

Beech   Ash   Hazel   Lime   Maple   Oak

▶ During the Spring the buds of deciduous trees, such as this oak, open up as the leaves inside grow. Sugars are quickly made in the leaves by photosynthesis, using the stronger sunlight. This process allows the tree to grow. Different trees come into leaf at different times. There is a saying which can be used to predict what the weather is going to be like in the Spring to come. "If the oak before the ash, we'll have a splash. If the ash before the oak, we'll be soaked". Watch oak and ash trees as they come into leaf, and see if the saying is true.

Animals in the Spring

As the Spring days become longer, many more animals become active. Animals prepare their homes to be ready for their young when they are born. The migrant birds which have spent the Winter in warmer places return to their breeding grounds to join the resident birds in nest building. Cold-blooded creatures emerge from their Winter hibernation as their body temperature rises with the surrounding warmth.

When it rains, animals cannot pull on coats and boots as people do. They have other ways of coping. Mammals have grease in their fur, so that the rain runs off instead of soaking in and making the fur soggy. Bird feathers work in a similar way, and birds spend much time preening (oiling their feathers).

Staying dry — mammal

Staying dry — bird

Marking the Boundary

A dog (male) fox marks out the boundaries of his territory by leaving scent. The sense of smell is much less good in humans than in many mammals. Do this experiment to see if you would survive well as a fox. Use a bottle of strong-smelling liquid, such as vinegar or vanilla. Ask a friend to shake a trail of drops across an open space while you are not looking. Now try to find the trail by crawling about, sniffing hard. Mark the point where you find the trail and then start again. Keep marking when you smell the trail and see if you can locate the territory of your "rival."

▲ These male oryx are fighting to decide which one will claim a certain territory, and the females within it.

Tree-top Territories

In a single tree, many animals will build a home and rear a family. Often a mammal or bird will hold a **territory**. This is an area which the animal will defend against other animals of the same kind. The territory will be large enough to provide enough food for the new family, and the home or nest will be somewhere in the middle. Some animals, on the other hand, nest together in communities, or colonies.

A male thrush sings from various points in his territory to warn off other thrushes. He will fight off any rivals who come too close. Try making a nest using twigs, leaves, moss, and other natural materials as a thrush does. During the Winter months a squirrel makes a drey close to the tree trunk. In the Spring a new one is built farther out in the branches, and this is where the young are born.

Look on wet days for frogs, snails, and slugs, and in damp places for woodlice. The problem for these animals in the Summer will not be avoiding the rain, but keeping cool and damp.

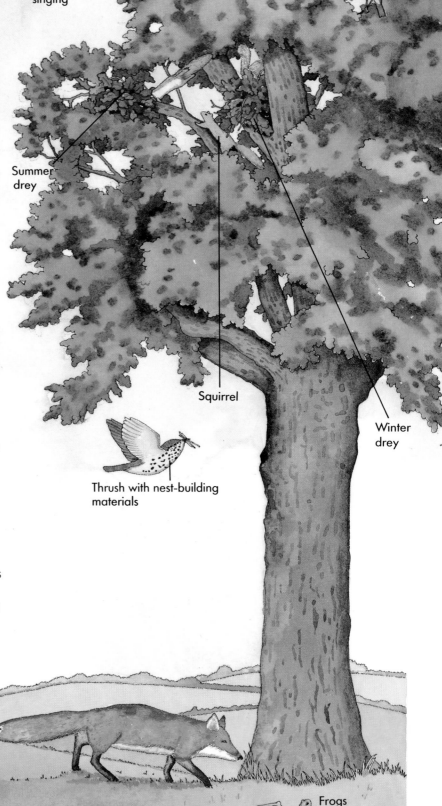

Male thrush singing

Summer drey

Squirrel

Winter drey

Thrush with nest-building materials

Foxes

Frogs

Nettle Soup and Hawthorn Nibbles

Equipment: 1 onion—peeled and chopped, 1 potato—peeled and chopped, cooking oil, salt and pepper, yogurt, stock cube, 20 nettles.

Oil
Salt Pepper Potato
Stock cube
Onion
Nettles
Use gloves!

Collect young nettle shoots from a clean place, wearing rubber gloves. Fry the onion and potato in cooking oil for a few minutes in a saucepan. Chop the leaves off the nettle stalks and add them to the saucepan with the stock cube and a quart of water. Boil until the potato is cooked. Sieve or ask an adult to liquidize the broth, then stir in seasoning and yogurt if required.

Young hawthorn leaves make a good addition to salads, and they can also be eaten in a sandwich. They should be washed first.

Hawthorn leaves

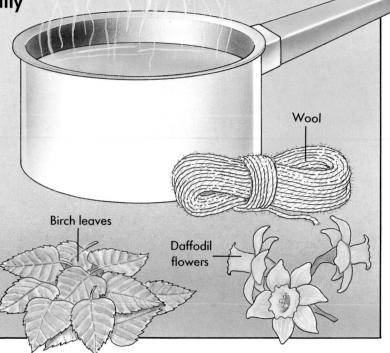

Dyeing Naturally

The color of the season can be captured by dyeing wool. To do this you will need an <u>old</u> saucepan (you may not be able to clean it afterward!). Use either white wool or cotton. Collect one of the plants illustrated, or experiment with other brightly-colored plants (you could try tree bark, yellow lichens, or blackberries). Boil the plant in a little water. When the water is well colored, cool it and strain the plants off. Now add the white wool and simmer until it has picked up the color.

Wool
Birch leaves
Daffodil flowers

Decorated Eggs

It is the custom in many places to decorate eggs in the Spring. Eggs remind people of the new life that appears in the Spring. To make a decorated chicken egg to keep, you must first blow it as described. Rinse the inside with water, then decorate the egg using paints or pens. Make stencil shapes with sticky tape to color around, then peel them off.

▶ Blowing an egg can be difficult. Make a hole with a pin in each end of a chicken egg. Blow into one hole to force the contents into a bowl.

Pin holes at either end

After a bird has built its nest, the eggs are laid. These are incubated (kept warm), usually by the parents, until the young birds hatch out.

People used to collect the eggs of wild birds for food, or sometimes just because they looked pretty. This is no longer permitted. Some birds have become very rare because no young birds have been left to hatch out. If you know where a bird is nesting, don't draw attention to it, and don't disturb the nest.

WARNING! some plants are poisonous — always check with an adult before you eat any flowers or leaves.

Glazed Flowers

Many plants make flowers in the Spring. They are often brightly colored to attract the insects which will pollinate them. Once pollination has taken place, seeds can start to form, and these will grow into next year's plants. This is why it is important not to pick wild flowers, because if a plant loses its flower it will also lose its seeds for the following year. Ask if you can have a few petals from garden flowers to make these glazed flowers. If you use garden primroses or roses you can eat them afterward—but remember that some flowers are poisonous.

Separate an egg white from the yolk. Beat the white with a fork, adding a little water until the liquid is just thin enough to use as a paint. Use a new, soft paintbrush to coat the petals with the egg white. Dip the petals in confectioners' sugar and leave them to dry.

Summer

At this time of the year a lot of sunlight energy is available, so plants complete their growth. Plants and animals that need damp conditions may find it difficult to avoid drying out. Animals that are out during the day may have problems staying cool. Those that normally rely on the protective cover of darkness to feed often have to show themselves at dawn and dusk.

▲ In a drought the ground can become so dry that it shrinks, and cracks appear. The experiment on the opposite page shows you how to measure the depth of these cracks.

Heating up

On a sunny day use your hand to compare the temperature of grass with that of black Tarmac. Dark and dull objects absorb a lot of heat energy and so become hotter than light and shiny objects, which reflect most of the energy back. You can use this fact to make your own solar heater. Fill a plastic bottle with

water and check the temperature of the water. Put the bottle in a black plastic bag and leave it in the sun. Check the temperature of the water again after a few hours. Some people use the free energy from the sun to heat the water in their house by this method. It has an extra advantage—it does not cause pollution.

Water heats up much more slowly than most

materials. Test this by placing a tray of water next to a tray of sand in the sun. Check at intervals to see which feels warmer. The fact that the temperature of water does not change quickly is useful for underwater animals like fish. Before the water can become too hot for them during the day, the sun goes down and the water starts to cool again.

Hours of Sunshine

In the section on Spring weather you can make a bar chart to show the length of the day. However, even though the time between dawn and dusk might be 16 hours, the sun might actually shine for only six of those hours. You could count the hours of sunshine with a stopwatch, but here is an easier way.

Make a chart, with two columns. Down the left-hand column mark the following times: 7·00, 8·30, 10·00, 11·30, 13·00, 14·30, 16·00, 17·30, 19·00, 20·30. During one day record whether the sun was shining (√) or not shining (×) at each of these times. To find out how sunny the day was, add up the number of ticks, and multiply by ten. For example, if you have four ticks, the day was approximately 40 percent sunny. For animals such as butterflies, the amount of sunshine in a day is more important than the length of the day.

The Dry Season

Although there may be a lot of rain in the Summer, most of the moisture quickly evaporates into the air. As a result, the ground can become so dry that it starts to crack. If you find a drought crack, tie a heavy weight onto a piece of string and lower it into the crack. Mark the string when the weight reaches the bottom and measure the length. Check each day to see if the crack gets deeper.

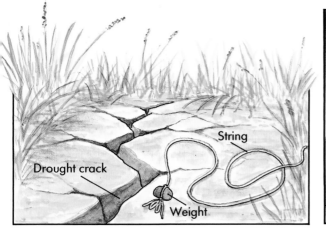

Drought crack

String

Weight

Summer Storms

Summer is a time of sudden storms. Huge movements of air are caused when some areas of ground heat up more quickly than others. Large, towering clouds form, and sparks of electricity flash across the sky. A lot of rain may fall in a short time. Mammals can often sense a thunderstorm long before it is heard or seen. They become restless, and their fur stands on end.

Sweaty Grass!

Plants use energy from the sun to make food in their green leaves. To do this they need to absorb water from the soil into their roots. Surplus water is **transpired** (breathed out) from the leaves. On a sunny day, place a plastic sheet on a lawn. Look under it at hourly intervals to see how much transpired water has collected on the sheet. To find out where grass gets water from when there is no rain, put the sheet out again, but overnight. On clear nights dew forms on the ground, and this provides a little extra water for plants.

Leaves in the Summer

The fact that leaves transpire so much water can cause problems for plants during a drought. However, some plants are well suited to living in dry places. Cacti lose very little water through transpiration, and can survive for years with hardly any water.

Trees are so large they transpire more water than most other plants, sometimes many gallons in a day. You can observe how water moves through a leaf in the following way. Pick a leafy deciduous twig and place it in a small amount of water mixed with red

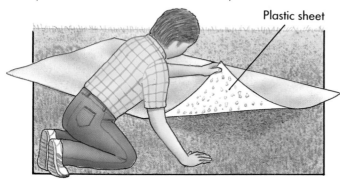

Plastic sheet

Cacti

Coping with Drought

Often, gardeners only water their plants every few days to encourage the plants to send down deeper roots looking for water. Try this experiment to see if this works. In one plastic box put a thin layer of absorbent cotton. Fill a second box with loose layers of cotton. Add cress seeds to both and water until they have germinated. Then keep the seeds in the first box damp, but put water into the bottom of the second box only when the cotton is nearly dry. After a week check to see what has happened to the roots.

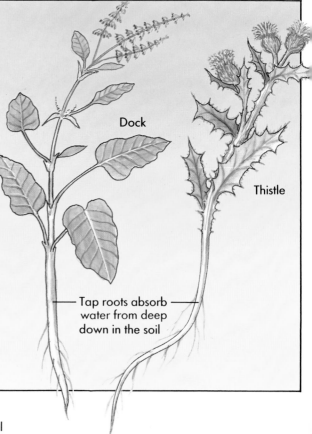

Dock

Thistle

Tap roots absorb water from deep down in the soil

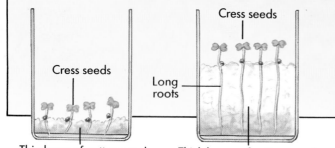

Cress seeds

Cress seeds

Long roots

Thin layer of cotton wool

Thick layers of cotton wool

cochineal dye. As the red color of the dye moves up the leaf it will show you where the water goes.

Leaves contain thousands of boxes to move water and food around. These boxes are easiest to see in old, fallen leaves in the Autumn. However, you can speed up the process of decay by putting Summer leaves in a bucket of water. Change the water if it starts to smell. The green part of the leaves will slowly rot away, leaving the veins behind. The pattern of veins is the "leaf skeleton."

Veins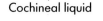

Cochineal liquid

Deciduous leaves

► The leaves of this oak tree are making sugars quickly, using the sunlight of the long days. The oak tree is now transpiring hundreds of gallons of water a day. This must be replaced by absorbing water from the soil through the roots. If there is drought the tree may have to lose its leaves early to save water. The tree now has flowers. Some of these flowers will be pollinated and develop into seeds.

Animals in the Summer

In the early Summer many animals give birth to eggs or young. Often the young must be fed and guarded, and the adults are kept busy day and night. Some animals are active only during the day; these are known as **diurnal** animals. If the temperature becomes too high during the day, this can cause problems. Warm-blooded creatures must keep a constant temperature and can become too hot. Mammals lose heat by sweating or panting. As water evaporates from the skin or tongue, the body cools down.

Life by Day

Many insects are diurnal. Butterflies and dragonflies need energy from the heat of the sun to be able to fly. Most flowers, therefore, open in the day to attract diurnal insects to pollinate them.
Amphibians, such as frogs and newts, shelter in sunny weather to stop themselves drying out. Reptiles, such as snakes and lizards, sun themselves to raise their body temperature and make themselves more active.

Buddleia

Kestrel

Cranefly

Caterpillars

Dog

Butterflies

Thrush   Daisies   Dragonfly   Rabbit

Hidden Nightlife

Many animals are active only at night. They are known as **nocturnal** animals. You can reveal some of this nighttime activity by making a pitfall trap.

Dig a hole in the ground and place an old jar in it so that the top is level with the soil. Cover the jar with a piece of wood raised on four stones to keep any rain out. Put some damp soil, leaves, and bark in the jar. In the morning check the trap to see what creatures have wandered past in the night and fallen in. Remember to set them free afterward!

Life by Night

Many creatures use the cover of darkness to move around more safely. Moths drink nectar from flowers that open specially at night to attract them. Small mammals, such as mice and voles, are active too. However, life at night is not completely safe. Predators make use of the cover of darkness. Bats use "echo location" (see page 31) to find insects. Owls have excellent sight and hearing. Foxes use their fine sense of smell to track down small animals.

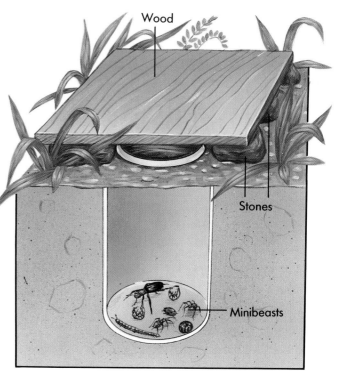

Wood

Stones

Minibeasts

Bat

Owl

Moth

Fox

Night-scented stock

Daisies close up at night

Stoats hunt day and night

Rabbits graze during the day and night

Lavender Baskets

In Summer most plants produce flowers which attract insects. When an insect visits a flower, pollination can occur and next year's seeds will start to form. Insects are attracted to flowers by their bright colors and sweet scents. You can capture the smell of lavender by making a "lavender basket."

Collect 11 lavender flowers, with 12 inches of stem still attached. Cut a yard length of half-inch-wide ribbon. Secure the base of the flower heads (1). Bend the stems back over the flower heads so that the flowers are enclosed within the stems (2). Weave the ribbon inside one stem, then outside the next, and so on around the length of the stems. Finish off with a bow in the ribbon (3).

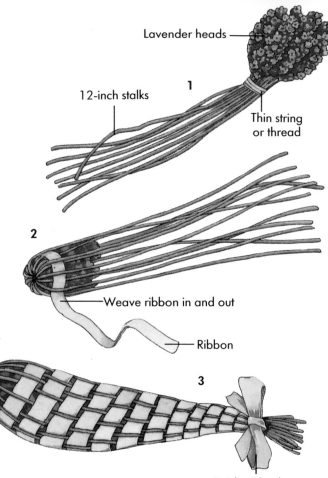

Lavender heads

12-inch stalks

1

Thin string or thread

2

Weave ribbon in and out

Ribbon

3

Finish with a bow

After Flowers

The reason why plants make flowers often only becomes clear in the Autumn. Monitor a flower to see what happens—a rose would be a good choice. Gently tie a bright piece of thread around the stem of the flower. Examine the flower every few days to see what happens after the petals fall off. Look to see where the seeds are starting to develop.

Mint Tea

Strong-smelling plants are sometimes used as foods or medicines. Try this refreshing Summer drink, using a common Summer plant. Wash a bunch of mint leaves and put them in a tea pot. Add some green tea for a stronger brew. Add hot water and leave the tea to infuse for a few minutes before pouring.

Mint leaves

Make a Flapping Butterfly

Trace the three pieces shown here onto cardboard, making two copies of the wing. Decorate the wing, then cut the four pieces out. Hinge the wings to the body using sticky tape at A and B. Make two holes in each wing and use these to hang the wings from the holes C and D in the strip of cardboard, using thin string. Attach a straw to the body at E from underneath. This can be pushed gently to make the wings flap. Hang the strip of cardboard up by string using holes C and D again. By taping heavy coins to the wings you should be able to make the butterfly flap more slowly, and for longer, when you let go.

Holes in wing

Summer is a good time to look for butterflies. They divide their time between feeding on nectar from flowers, breeding, and laying eggs, and sunning themselves.

E

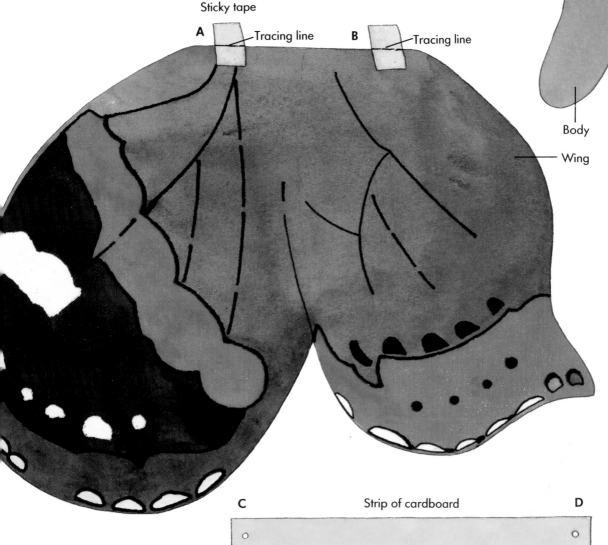

Sticky tape

A — Tracing line   B — Tracing line

Body

Wing

C   Strip of cardboard   D

Autumn

As Autumn draws in the days become shorter, and there is less energy from the sun for plants and animals to use. The nights may be cold and frosty, and dew often forms overnight. Plants and animals prepare for the Winter. Many will die. However, during the Autumn dead things are recycled into the soil, so the nutrients can be used again next year.

Condensing Water

If a cold night follows a warm Autumn day, **condensation** will occur. To see condensation for yourself, put a glass jar in a refrigerator for 30 minutes, then remove it to a warm place. The water that condenses on the glass was present in the warm air all along — but it was invisible until the air cooled.

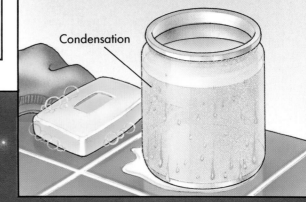

Condensation

 ## Star Gazing

The night sky is often very clear in Autumn. If you have binoculars, look at the moon to see the craters. (You must <u>never</u> look at the sun through binoculars — it will blind you.) Many newspapers have maps every month to help you to identify the star groupings, or constellations. Because the earth is spinning around, the stars appear to move slowly across the sky. Only the North Star appears to stay in the same place in the sky, because it is positioned directly above the North Pole. When birds are migrating between countries they use the North Star to find their direction. Sailors, too, use stars to navigate across the oceans. People used to think that swallows migrated to the moon — 238,862 miles away! In fact, the record for migration goes to the arctic tern which can travel right around the earth each year — a distance of about 25,000 miles.

Games in Fog and Dew

When warm air outside condenses overnight on the ground, a morning **dew** is the result. If the dew freezes then it is called **frost**. Sometimes water condenses in the air itself, causing **fog** or **mist**.

Fog is a great challenge to birds, especially if they are migrating. Next time it is foggy play this game in a park or playground to find out why. Ask a friend to stand still. Walk away from them until they are well out of sight. Now try to find them again by walking in a straight line. Try again, but this time call at intervals. Ask your friend to echo your call. This is how bats find prey to eat in the dark. They make a high pitched noise which bounces back off insects, helping the bat to home in on its prey. This is called "**echo location**."

▼ If dew has formed, look to see if there are any wild animal tracks.

What is Soil?

During the Summer, plants take in the goodness, or **nutrients**, from the soil as they grow. If this continued happening throughout the year, the soil would lose all its nutrients and nothing would be able to grow in it. On the next page you can find out how nutrients are returned to the soil. If you do the experiment here you can discover what soil is made of. Half fill a jar with soil and top it up with water. Screw the lid on tightly, shake the jar well and leave the contents to settle. The humus on top is the dead matter which provides nutrients in the soil. Sand and clay provide structure to the soil. Stones help the water to drain away, so that the soil does not become waterlogged.

Humus

Water

Sand

Mud or clay

Small stones

Larger stones

► In the Autumn, deciduous trees lose their leaves. Many other plants die back. Some animals die as the weather gets colder and food becomes short. What happens to all these dead things? Fortunately there are plants and animals which feed on decaying matter. Animals which do this are called **scavengers**. Plants which live off dead matter include the **fungi**. These do not make their own food like many plants. Instead fungi absorb nutrients from dead things through their roots. You can grow fungi by keeping stale bread wet. The mold which appears is a type of fungus. Some fungi, such as mushrooms, can be eaten. However, some are extremely poisonous. The fungus in the picture is feeding off dead wood.

The Natural Way to Throw Away

In a garden or field nutrients are removed from the ground each time vegetables or flowers are picked. You can help to return nutrients to the soil by making a compost heap. Dead leaves, vegetable peelings, rotten fruit, and grass cuttings can all be turned into compost. The "rotters," such as fungi, and scavenger animals, such as worms, will feed on the dead matter breaking it down. When the decay is complete, the compost can be dug into the garden soil to replace the lost nutrients.

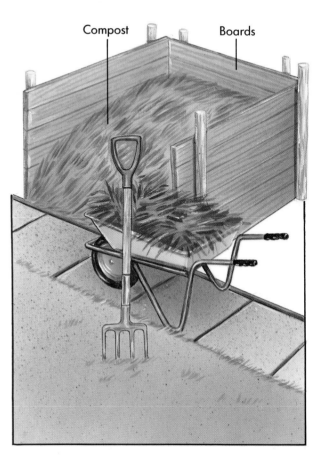

Compost   Boards

Falling Leaves

You can monitor how deciduous trees lose their leaves by choosing a particular branch on a deciduous tree. Mark 20 leaves with bright paint. Every few days record how many of the marked leaves have fallen off. Try marking leaves on different types of deciduous trees to find out which type loses its leaves first. Look for leaf scars on a twig. This is where the leaves were attached to the twig, and is the point where the water supply to the leaf was cut off, causing the leaf to die.

▲ Find out what happens to dead leaves by pinning some to the ground using wire netting.

Mark leaves with paint

Leaf scar

▶ Deciduous trees, such as this oak tree, often look very colorful in the Autumn. Photosynthesis in the leaves stops, and the green chlorophyl which captured the energy of the sun breaks down. The tree is covered with acorns, which are seeds. Many of these will be eaten by birds or mammals, but a few may germinate. In a hundred years they may grow into a new oak tree like the one here.

Autumn Preparations

At this time of the year animals start to prepare for the hard Winter months. Food will be difficult to find, so many animals store food to eat later in the Winter. Most mammals grow a thicker Winter coat. It is a traditional time for humans to burn garbage, but if possible it is better that leaves and other dead plants are made into compost. If you do have a fire, remember to check it for any hibernating animals before setting light to it.

Closing Down for the Winter

In preparation for Winter, many animals eat lots of food and then find a place to hibernate, often under the soil. Many winged insects will die because in cold weather they cannot fly well enough to find food. However, there will be insect eggs, larvae, and pupae ready to hatch into new adult insects when the Spring comes. Animals that eat insects will have to change their feeding habits or lifestyles in the Winter, or they will starve. Some birds change their diet and eat seeds instead. Others migrate to countries where insects are still available.

Bats hibernate in a roost where they lower their body temperature to save energy. They must not be disturbed or they will lose vital energy which they then cannot replace. Snails seal over the entrance to their shell. It is not harmful to bring these into the warm to wake up. Give them some fresh leaves to eat before putting them back where you found them.

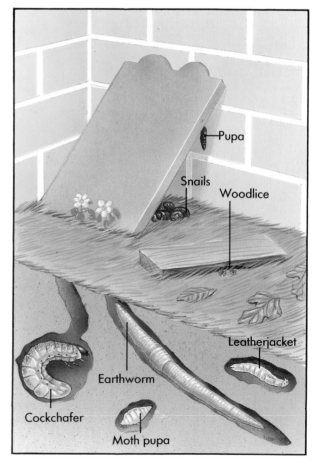

Pupa
Snails
Woodlice
Leatherjacket
Earthworm
Cockchafer
Moth pupa

Stocking Up for the Winter

Many plants produce seeds at this time of year. Often these are in the form of berries and nuts which animals will eat and collect, and so spread around. Hide some nuts in different places outside and see if you can find them the next day, and then next week. Flocks of birds strip fruit bushes bare. Some mammals form a thick layer of fat under their skin. This will be used later to provide energy, and will help to insulate the animal from the cold. In very cold weather, many warm-blooded creatures will die. They will not be able to find enough food to provide energy to stay warm.

Elderberry

Blackberry

Jay

Holly berry

Fox

Chestnut

Fir cone

Acorn

Humans Stocking Up

Equipment: 1 pound apples, 1 pound blackberries, 2 pounds sugar, lemon, water.

People lay down fat in the Winter too! They also store food. Autumn fruit can be preserved as jam. Try making this blackberry and apple jam with an adult. Wash and chop 1 pound of apples, including the peel and core. Add half pint of water and simmer to a pulp. Cool the pulp and squeeze it through muslin. Add 1 pound of blackberries and the juice of one lemon, together with 2 pounds of sugar. Heat the mixture gently, stirring until the sugar has dissolved. Then boil until it is thick. Take great care because the jam becomes very hot. To check it is ready, put a little on a cold saucer — a skin should form. Pour the jam into warmed pots, and cover with wax disks. Seal tightly with a lid, or cellophane and a rubber band. All sorts of fruits can be used to make jam.

► The earth is tilted slightly in relation to the sun. During the Summer months, the northern hemisphere (half) of the earth is facing the sun more directly. As a result more sunlight energy reaches the surface of the earth. At the same time the southern hemisphere is tilted away from the sun and so has Winter. Six months later the situation is reversed. While the northern hemisphere has Winter, it is Summer in the southern hemisphere.

Plants and animals have ways of living to cope with the changing seasons, as you have seen in this book. They have often developed over time to follow the seasonal pattern of one particular area. Many people are concerned that if the weather patterns of the earth change rapidly due to human activity some plants and animals will not be able to adapt and survive in the new conditions.

Waste not, Want not

Autumn is the time when dead things are recycled into the soil. If this recycling stopped, dead leaves would soon swamp everything and the soil would lose its goodness. Unfortunately, people do not recycle things in the same way. Trees are cut down to make paper which is then thrown into garbage dumps. Waste vegetable matter is thrown away instead of being turned into compost and returned to the soil. Glass is made from sand and then dumped. Metal ore is dug up and made into cans which are discarded. At the same time, energy is wasted and pollution caused. Find out how much of your garbage could be recycled and then follow the example of Nature!

Cans

Gla

Newspaper

Thistle Mice

Some of the seeds made by plants in the Autumn make attractive decorations. However, don't take too many because animals need them for food to stay alive.

To make these thistle mice, break off the scales from the fir cone and dip the ends in glue. Stick these into the thistle head to make ears and feet. Make eyes and a nose by pressing in the seeds. Use a length of string to make the tail.

The seeds used here are all scattered in different ways. Thistle heads have tiny hooks which cling on to mammals' fur. Poppy seeds are contained in a "pepper pot" head which shakes out the seeds. Fir cones open on fine days, and then the seeds hidden by its scales are blown away.

Equipment: a thistle head (or other prickly seed head), a fir cone, large black seeds (for example, poppy seeds), string, glue.

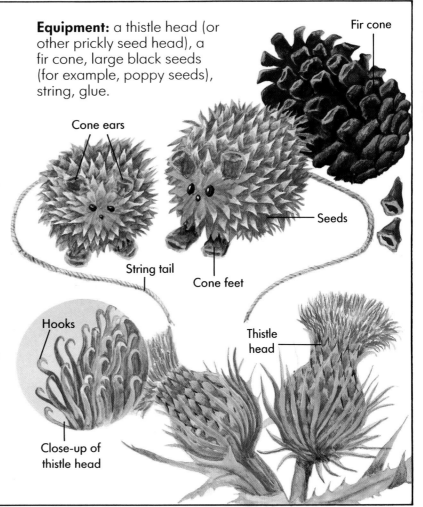

Fir cone

Cone ears

Seeds

String tail

Cone feet

Hooks

Close-up of thistle head

Thistle head

The Cycle Continues

People often think that Autumn is the end of the year. Many birds leave for warmer countries. Some animals prepare to hibernate. Most insects die. Deciduous trees shed their leaves. Many plants make seeds and then die back. However, there is no beginning or end to the cycle of the seasons. Autumn is also the time when ivy comes into flower, providing food for remaining insects. The fruits and seeds everywhere will grow into

plants next year. It is the rutting time for deer — the young will be born in the Spring. Take an Autumn amble and look for signs that the seasonal cycle is continuing.

Bees

Mild days, frosty nights

Dragonfly nymphs, and **poppy seeds** are well suited to surviving the winter.
Dragonfly adults and **poppy flowers**: DIE.
Swallows: any left will STARVE.

Harsh frost

Poppy flower, dragonfly adult and **swallow**: DIE.
Badger and **thrush**: *back 1 space.*
Swallow: STARVES

Snow thaws

A square to res
before the seas
cycle continu

Deep snow
Food covered up.

Thrush, dragonfly (adult only), **poppy** (flower only): DIE.
Swallow: all swallows should have migrated. Any left will STARVE.

WINTER

Surviving the Seasons

Choose an animal or plant, and see if y
can last a whole year as you battle to
survive the seasons. Up to six people co
play. Cut out rectangles of card, an inc
half an inch to make a counter for each
player. Write (or draw) on each counte
of these: **Oak, Poppy Seed, Thrush, Swallow, Dragonfly Nymph, Badger.** C
the reverse of the poppy seed counter v
Poppy Flower. You will be instructed wh
to turn the counter over to show when t
seed has grown and flowered; and whe
turn it back again to show when the flov
has made seeds. On the reverse of the
dragonfly nymph counter write **Dragon
Adult.** You will be instructed when the
dragonfly changes from one stage of its

Hedge cut
Hedges provide food for animal life.

Oak: new growth cut back. *Move back 2 spaces.*
Thrush: STARVE because no berries to eat.
Badger: food shortage. *Move back 2 spaces.*

Humans provide food

Thrush and **badger**: *move on 3 spaces.*

AUTUMN

Early frost
Plants and insects affected.

Poppy, dragonfly (adult only): KILLED.
Swallow: migrate to Africa for Winter. *Leave the game for 3 turns until Spring arrives then rejoin at the start point.*

Sunshine and showers
Good growing conditions.

Poppy: if at flower stage, makes seed. *Turn counter over.*
Dragonfly: adult lays egg to make nymphs. *Turn counter over.*

Drought
If water is short, suffers.

Thrush and **swa**
move back 1 s
Oak: *back 1 spc*
on first round.
trees need wo
Dragonfly nymp
DIES when the
dries out.

Start point

Spring weather

SPRING

Nature Reserve
All wildlife is protected here.

Move your counter on 2 spaces.

Shooters and trappers
Animal life at risk.

Thrush SHOT
Swallow SHOT
Badger TRAPPED

Warm sunny weather
Plants and animals can grow quickly.

Poppy seed can grow into flower. *Turn the counter over.*
Dragonfly nymph hatches into adult dragonfly. *Turn the counter over.*

Late frost
Insects and plants may die.

Swallow: no insects to feed on, so you STARVE.
Poppy: if you are at the flower stage you are KILLED. or: if you are a seed you survive.
Badger: delay breeding. *Move back 1 space.*

Continuous wet weather
This affects animal life.

Thrush: DIE of cold if this is your first circuit of the board. Most birds die in their first year.
Dragonfly: DIE if adult. Dragonfly nymph survives.

le to another. All pieces start at the ginning of Spring. Put three coins in a jar. e turns to shake out the coins. For each n that turns up "heads", move one are. For example if you score two heads d one tail, you move two squares. If you re three tails you stay where you are! d the square to see if there is an ruction for your piece. If you have to ve forward or back, remember to read instructions on the new square you ne to as well. If the instruction is in PITAL LETTERS your animal or plant has en killed. Start again, with a new piece if u like. See which piece is the first to nplete a whole year, and which one es around the most times.

SUMMER

arm showery weather

r: seed grows into er. *Turn counter r. or: flower es seed. Turn nter over.*
onfly: nymph hes into adult. counter over. or: t lays egg. Turn nter over.*

Poison sprayed on gardens and fields

Thrush, swallow, and **badger** become ill. *Move back 1 space and miss a turn in the wildlife area.*
Oak: POISONED if on first circuit. Young trees are easily killed.
Dragonfly (adult or nymph): POISONED.

Wildlife area made at school
Wildlife can flourish.

All counters move on 2 spaces.

Index

Editor: Nicky Barber
Designer: Ben White
Illustrators: Oxford Illustrators
Liz Peperell,
Kuo Kang Chen

Cover Design: Terry Woodley
Picture Research: Elaine Willis

The publishers wish to thank the following for supplying photographs for this book:

Page 7 ZEFA; 9 ZEFA; 17 ZEFA; 18 NHPA/Nigel Dennis; NHPA/Anthony Bannister; 25 ZEFA; 32 NHPA/Stephen Dalton; 33 ZEFA; 36 Science Photo Library.

Library of Congress Cataloging-in-Publication Data
Harlow, Rosie
    Cycles and seasons / Rosie Harlow and Gareth Morgan
        p.   cm. —(Fun with science)
    Includes index.
    Summary: Uses simple experiments to demonstrate why the seasons happen and how they affect living things, migration, weather cycles, and human adaptations.
    ISBN 0–531–19123–0
    1. Seasons—Experiments—Juvenile literature.
    2. Meterology—Periodicity—Experiments—Juvenile literature. (1. Seasons—Experiments.
    2. Experiments.)
    I. Morgan, Gareth   II. Title.   III. Series.
    QB637.4.M67   1991   91–2567
    525'.5'078—dc20   CIP
                                                    AC